The Very First Christmas

The Very First Christmas

Tellwell Talent
www.tellwell.ca

ISBN
978-1-77370-556-9 (Hardcover)
978-1-77370-557-6 (Paperback)
978-1-77370-555-2 (eBook)

Dear Readers,

On Christmas morning, like virtually every other day, my husband and I rose early to another clear blue sky. Celebrating this holiday in a foreign country without family and festivities seemed empty and forlorn; so, to kill time and to get out of our home, we took a drive out into the desert and gave our dogs a good run. As the sun peeked over the horizon in the east, its rays still gentle and soft, the moon, aglow in the morning light, descended over the barren landscape to the west. I stood atop a sand dune in the middle of the Arabian Peninsula. With the wind whipping at my abaya and the sand stinging my ankles, my gaze scanned the skyline and took in the void of any sign of civilization. Looking towards the heavens, I was surprised to see stars still visible in the early dawn. I found myself drifting back in time. Could it be possible that one of the wise men had stood in this very spot as he travelled to Bethlehem? An incredible peace washed over me and the glamour of the Christmas I was missing filled with roast turkey, decorated trees, gifts, and family disappeared. At that moment the true Christmas, just as it may have happened over two thousand years ago, filled first with dust and desert heat, fear and heartache, and then finally peace and joy, was revealed. This is the inspiration for the story you read here.

MARY

EVEN now, recalling those first days of her pregnancy brought on an ache that made her chest tighten, her chin quiver, and the tears rise in her eyes. Like so many other nights, the anticipation of her upcoming nuptials had Mary so excited that trying to sleep had been impossible. Her betrothal to the son of a family as fine as Joseph's was an answer to many years of prayer, and her family was consumed with preparations. Slipping quietly from her mat so as not to disturb her little sister blissfully snoring next to her, Mary had tiptoed to the window to stare out at the little town she called home. Gazing up at the stars in the night sky and the vast heavens above, she had whispered her gratitude to the Almighty for the thousandth time. That Joseph was from a respected family was an immense blessing, but his genuine kindness and caring was the gift that Mary appreciated the most. As a young girl, she had frequently watched the boys play on the street, and she had never forgotten how Joseph would always ensure that the younger boys would get to take a turn. He would cheer on their efforts, and take care that they were safe. Watching over those boys even though they were not part of his family had shown Mary that Joseph respected others. That their marriage had the potential to be a happy one seemed almost too good to be true. Leaning forward against the rough-hewn wood of the window frame, she was oblivious to its tiny slivers pressing into her slender arm as she closed her eyes and dreamed about her future. With visions of a happy family dancing around in her mind, she'd dozed lightly while the cool night breeze gently blew wisps of her fine black hair back from her face.

Startled into the present by a piercing and commanding voice calling her name, Mary's eyes had flung open only to be blinded by a light so bright she had drawn her hands to her face to shield herself from the intensity. Peering through the slits between her fingers she was astonished by the image of a winged golden sentinel floating just outside the window. Enveloping her with his smile when their gazes met, he moved in still closer. Mesmerized by the messenger's radiance that seemed to pulse with life, Mary stood rooted to the floor. Reaching his hands heavenward, he proclaimed the Holiest of the

Almighty. Then, in a softer and gentler tone, he explained to Mary that she had been shown great favour and was to become pregnant. The Lord of all had selected her to be the mother of the Son of God.

Stunned, Mary remained motionless as the angel retreated from the window and disappeared in the heavens. Finally coming to her senses, she quickly turned to check her little sister's reaction. Amazingly, she found Fatima still sound asleep. She might have ordinarily found the girl's blissful oblivion to be an amusing story to share with her parents in the morning, but right now Mary wished Fatima had been awake to witness the event. Her corroboration could be the only thing that would possibly make Mary's story believable. Stepping into the large room next to hers she had found her parents sleeping peacefully. How could they have slumbered through the envoy's commanding voice? Why had she been the only one to see him? Surely the angel would share this incredible news with everyone? Without any witnesses, Mary knew no one would believe her.

She rushed back to the window and searched the heavens for further sign of the angel. Understanding he was gone, she leaned against her familiar perch for support and wrapped her arms around her still flat belly. How could it be true? Why would God choose a woman as simple as her to be part of such a magnificent plan? Overwhelmed, she stood there, her emotions tearing her in every direction. Joy mixed with fear and trepidation, and she considered the ramifications of the angel's news. As tears filled her eyes, through her blurred vision she witnessed the sun's first rays reaching over the horizon. Rosy light washed over her face, and she closed her eyes. And as the sun's rays warmed her skin, a feeling of intense awe flowed through her. Her legs began to tremble as the wonder of the privilege took root in her heart. She had been chosen as the mother of the Messiah. A small smile lifted the corners of her mouth and her face was transformed by a deep peace settling over her.

As the months passed by Mary did her best to endure her emotional turmoil with hope. She held fast to her belief that God would surprise her again, this time announcing to everyone her great blessing. Night after night she waited for the angel's return. But over time, as she sat looking out the same window she had that first morning, her confidence gave out. Pulling her knees up to her chest, she protectively embraced the new life that she could no longer deny was growing within her. With her body beginning to show the signs of her pregnancy her ability to hide the truth would soon be over. She would have to tell her parents. Mary knew that even a man and woman as faithful as her father and mother would have difficulty believing. They would be devastated, for their daughter was pregnant out of wedlock. Her father's business would suffer greatly, thereby threatening their livelihood. Her mother would be cast out of the circle of women she presently held close, and young Fatima would lose all chances of finding a reputable husband. At the very moment she had been thanking God for her husband to be, her future with him had been snatched from her grasp. There was no possible way he would consider their marriage now. Even Mary's future in her own family was suddenly as precarious as a dewdrop on the end of a fig tree leaf.

JOSEPH

JOSEPH cringed inwardly while almost unconsciously the corners of his mouth turned up into a mischievous grin. Even now, while thinking back and wondering if he had always been so vain or if the betrothal process was to blame, he had trouble resisting his self-admiration. The first son of a family of fine reputation, he was desirable husband material. Trained by his father, he was a skilled carpenter with a secure future in the family business. He had found it all quite laughable as the parents of each of the respective young ladies did their best to sway his mother in their favour. His friends would look at him enviously and he found himself walking around town with a swagger in his walk and his chin lifted a little higher in response to all the attention.

He had taken only a slight interest in the various girls, knowing that regardless of what he wanted he would be expected to fulfil his mother's wishes on the matter. When she had told him that she was favouring Mary, he had been a little surprised. He had expected his mother to choose one of the girls from the families of higher stature, but her intent became clear when she explained that Mary conducted herself in a respectful manner that she believed would blend into their family nicely. Joseph had realized that his mother meant to keep the upper hand in the household. Though not overly concerned, he sought out his sister early one morning and asked for her thoughts on the matter. She had been ecstatic. Apparently, she was not overly fond of the other girls with their conceited and pompous attitudes. She had been hoping their mother would choose Mary so she wouldn't have to live with one of those other girls.

Contrary to her usual demure poise, Mary seemed very enthusiastic and eager at the large party that his mother had hosted to share their announcement of betrothal. Joseph clearly remembered showing off that evening. Catching Mary's eye, he had juggled the empty wine goblets while watching her gaze grow from amusement into amazement. It wasn't until months later with Mary's sudden disappearance and her father's quiet insistence that the wedding be called off that Joseph had fully discovered the enormity of his ego. There was no way he could be humiliated by a broken engagement. Whatever the problem, Mary would not be given the option to turn him away now. Consumed by his pride he kept the news quiet. Night after night he lay in bed, unable to sleep, his fury growing deeper. Finally, utterly exhausted, he had fallen into a troubled sleep and dreamed. In his dream, an angel spoke to him, insisting that he take Mary, pregnant with God's own Son, as his wife. This dream disturbed Joseph greatly, and when he awoke he dispelled the idea as the result of overtiredness. But each night the angel returned until the dream literally consumed his thoughts. He threw himself into his work to try and distract his mind. Focusing on the wood in his hands, he examined the grain of the oxen yoke for the hundredth time to ensure the wood could hold the strength of the huge beast. He tried to avoid the reality of what his dream had conveyed.

Joseph was dumbfounded. Had the dream really been a message from God? Why would God ask him to throw away his future for Mary and a child he knew he was not the father of? Joseph's family followed the Hebrew rituals more out of habit than faith, but suddenly he wished he knew his Hebrew God better. He could vaguely recall a story from his bar mitzvah lessons that foretold of a baby Messiah, but since he had only given half of his attention to his studies, this recollection was hazy at best.

When he finally confessed his dream to his mother, she had quite easily shrugged off the angel's role. No doubt her son had been celebrating with perhaps just a little too much wine. Still, surmising her son was smitten with young Mary, she advised him it would be wise to see the betrothal through and marry the girl. She avoided any discussion of the girl's pregnancy, but presumed that Joseph's knowledge of the situation meant he was more involved than he was admitting. That Mary's parents had allowed the girl in Joseph's company unchaperoned was completely inappropriate - and a surprise, considering how strict her father had appeared to be with his eldest daughter. Regardless, she would not risk dishonouring her family with Joseph's uncontrolled desires. Whatever had gotten into him she was unsure, but his punishment for lack of good judgment in this instance would be harsh. There would be no more discussions until he talked to Mary's father and worked things out. Joseph was told that he would have to live with the consequences of his actions.

Joseph had gone to his mother seeking support, and so he was surprised by her lack of sympathy and quick assumption of his guilt. He had thought she would have been a stronger advocate for his well-being but it appeared that the family's reputation was even more important to her. Suddenly he felt very alone. Somehow, in a matter of a few weeks, he had gone from being on top of the world to a man with nothing left to lose.

Sun-Lin

Sun-Lin vividly recalled the day his future took its dramatic turn. His grandfather, Ming-Tan, had asked that he stay home that morning rather than join the other young men at the palace for their customary lessons. Grandfather, after immense training, reading, and studying, had provided many years of wise counsel to the Emperor. Over the last couple of weeks, Grandfather had become quite uncharacteristically excited. He had taken Sun-Lin aside on several occasions and advised him to be ready, for he had a grand plan for his grandson. Just the other night Grandfather had woken Sun-Lin in the middle of the night, taken him outside, and pointed out a bright new star in the sky. He shared that this star was an important sign and a guide for those who wanted to pay tribute to a great new King. Then, that very morning, Grandfather had told Sun-Lin to forego his studies and wait vigilantly for his return from his audience with the Emperor. Watching from the front stairs, Sun-Lin peered down the marble-lined corridor towards the Emperor's quarters. He had been watching for what felt like days. Patience had never been his strong suit. If not for his extraordinary imagination that had created figures and patterns from the variations in the polished stone at his feet, he would surely have given up and left his post hours ago.

Finally, his grandfather returned, practically stumbling up the stairs as he rushed by, and calling him to join him in his private quarters. Grandfather explained that the two of them would be going on a very significant and worthy journey. His lifetime of research and dedication would finally be rewarded. With the bright new star to follow, the time had come - as indicated by the many historical writings - to find and honour a new King. This King would reign as King of all Kings. The Emperor wanted to be sure that this King would view him in a favourable light, as an ally. Ming-Tan had been preparing for this moment for many years, silently watching those men who served the Emperor, looking for those who were not only skilled and accomplished, but honourable and dependable as well. That afternoon he gathered a group of warriors, interpreters, and explorers to accompany him on this historical quest. Their allegiance to the Emperor was paramount, as they would be responsible for Ming-Tan's and Sun-Lin's welfare along with safeguarding the great treasure they would carry with them. These chosen warriors and explorers were promised commendation in the history books and a great reward upon Ming's and Sun's safe return home. Ming had once hoped this opportunity would arise while he was still a fit young man, but now, as an aged old man, he saw a new opportunity. Sun-Lin would assist him and thus earn a spot in the history books as well.

Sun-Lin wasn't thrilled with the idea of spending weeks on end travelling with his grandfather, but on the other hand his classes at the palace were so exceptionally boring. He was constantly getting into trouble of one kind or another, and so anything would be better than this. When his grandfather had explained that the journey would be a true test of his character and would require more patience and perseverance than he had ever been asked of before, Sun-Lin had had his doubts. He secretly hadn't really cared if they even found this mighty King as just the idea of being off on an exciting adventure alongside great warriors and seasoned travellers sounded fantastic.

Tariq

Tariq's brilliant mind had been evident from the time he was just a young child. His wealthy merchant father would bring him along when he travelled the foreign lands in his search for goods to trade. By quickly picking up the unfamiliar languages and customs from the distant countries, he was constantly impressing his father and his father's business associates. While at home his father would hire tutors for Tariq, knowing it was important that he bring up an educated boy who could both read and manage money. Very impressed with his quick intellect and level of comprehension, his tutors had submitted his name as a candidate for apprenticeship with the local magi. When he was selected for a position to study with the Sheik's counsel, he had begged his father to let him accept the opportunity. From the earliest years under the counsel's tutelage, he had been fascinated with the writings about the singular Almighty God worshipped by the people in the northern land. Intrigued, he had read and studied everything available to him. He found the stories of the Messiah's return most captivating and he had taken up astronomy so he could watch for the star that would mark His arrival. He knew there had been other men before him who had shared his hope. He knew that hundreds of years had passed, and that hundreds more may yet come to pass, but if there was any chance of the Messiah's coming during his lifetime, Tariq wanted to be prepared. Poring over the scrolls, re-reading until he had them memorized, he couldn't think of a worthier calling than to be a part of this Great Event in man's history.

His father, who had never understood his love of studying, would frequently withdraw Tariq from school and drag his son along with him on a trip to one foreign land or another to ensure he had "worldly experience to go along with all his book learning". A firm believer of learning through experience, Tariq's father felt it was part of his duty to get his son's nose out of his scrolls - even if only a few times a year. Tariq found the trips interesting and enjoyed the opportunity these real-life experiences offered to substantiate his studies, but his father's lack of affirmation and endorsement of his schooling meant that Tariq was overlooked for counsel duties for several years. A position on the counsel was a coveted one, and so

Tariq had always considered his father's interference to be more of a curse than a blessing. He had frequently hoped that for one reason or another his father would give up and leave him alone. That is, until now. A bright new star had appeared in the night sky and though he may have been overlooked for many past honours, it was his previous travel experience as well as his in-depth studies of the Hebrews and their land that had made his selection for this important quest clear to everyone involved. He was the natural choice. So, while the other counsellors envied his position, there was little debate. He would be the one to make the trip. Even now, while he held the position of one of five key counsellors to the Sheik and was revered by all who knew him, he was certain that it was those trips with his father that had secured him this coveted role today. He pondered that fact and wondered if his father's interference had been providence all along. Was this trip more than fate or luck? His studies of the powerful Almighty God he was being sent to search out indicated it was so.

Elam

Elam couldn't remember a time when he hadn't known what he wanted to be. Fascinated by the stories of the land's great leaders, Elam had promised himself that one day he too would have stories passed down from generation to generation about his great achievements. Everything he had done from his childhood on had worked towards that goal. His youth had been divided between studying and assisting numerous influential and wealthy landowners and government officials, trying to prove his worth. At times, he had wished he were like the other boys. His younger brother Rafoul had spent his childhood dallying around, following any whim he so desired, never worrying about being held accountable for his actions. Elam had considered living in a more carefree way, without thinking about the impact that his decisions might have on his future, but it had been impossible. He could not change who he was, and he was driven to meet his desire with a consuming passion. One day, people would look up and honour him. One day, his name would become a part of history.

Now a grown man in the position of governor, his belief that his efforts would be recognized one day had come to glorious fruition. His charisma and caring had the people truly happy to be under his rule, and so united, they had achieved much to help improve living conditions for all. He was particularly proud of the recently completed irrigation system, as he was positive that this year's crop yields would be very impressive. He was confident that he was giving his citizens a better life. But were his efforts good enough to be recorded in history?

GABRIEL

DANCING from foot to foot, the angel Gabriel felt like he was going to explode from all his built-up energy. As usual, he was having difficulty not letting his anticipation get the better of him. He had always found it so hard to be patient, and when he was actively involved in one of the Lord's plans, patience was almost impossible. It was so incredibly exciting to watch things come together as a whole before him, each aspect complementing the others.

He felt a huge amount of empathy towards the children of the Earth, for he watched as they wrestled to be patient as well. Some would pray, struggling to know what the Father had planned for them, wanting to know what their futures held. Gabriel could identify with them, for he too was anxious to know what would happen. Still others would find themselves in situations that fulfilled God's plans without any knowledge of the Lord working in their lives. Gabriel always felt sorry for those poor souls. That they could go through each day without seeing the wonder of the Lord around them was so incredibly difficult to watch. He wanted to swoop down and proclaim the Lord's mightiness, and show them all His amazing handiwork on Earth and in the heavens.

No doubt they would have tried to make things happen their own way in their own time if they could. But the Father would wait until the perfect opportune moment before revealing His will to them. The very lack of their own input proved this was God's handiwork and not their own. Oh, how Gabriel loved to see everything fit together in the end.

The workings of the Lord were so mysterious that even Gabriel, an angel, struggled to see how everything worked together. However, he had realized long ago that the puzzle pieces were almost as important as the finished result. Having played an active part in many of the Lord's great events that had been marked down in human history, Gabriel knew that the Lord would even work man's disobedience into blessings and ignorance into revelation.

Chuckling, he could still vividly recall old Zechariah's face when he had been told he and Elizabeth would be parents. Fervent as he was, Zechariah did not believe, and so the Lord had tied his tongue until his son's birth to show him the error of his ways. The exuberant Gabriel was sure that he would have lost his own mind not being able to speak for so long, but at the same time he found it immensely satisfying to see the Lord stretch the limits of the earthly realm for his purpose. He watched the amazement and wonder rise up in His children. Yes, God knew how to get their attention, and yet many times, like now, he would quietly, almost invisibly, bring His will to the world. These were the moments where human faith really shone.

Gabriel's trips to Joseph night after night to convince the young man to wed Mary had not been a surprise. It was hard enough to satisfy doubt in even the most ardent believers, and Joseph's faith was weak and lacking a knowledgeable foundation. That Joseph, like many poor souls, had ultimately followed through with the Lord's plan based on an ulterior purpose was a common occurrence. The saving of his family's reputation and his own ego were apparently more important than seeking out the true purpose to his situation. In contrast, Mary's calm acceptance of her parental role suggested a much stronger woman than her quiet nature and youth let on - and Gabriel had been both surprised and impressed. Mary was evidently the perfect choice. Joseph, on the other hand, seemed less than fitting. Gabriel pondered what special skill the boy may hold that had caused the Lord to choose him.

Jophar

A simple shepherd boy, Jophar had never been a people person. Taunted and teased because of his disfigurement, his disappointment in people had begun early and ran deep. His father, a compassionate man, felt intense pain watching his little boy suffer. To alleviate the distress of simply living amongst his brothers and their friends, he had assigned his youngest son the task of shepherding a small herd of goats and sheep as soon as he was old enough to take on the responsibility. Jophar loved the fun-loving and mild-mannered animals. Up in the hills, he was blissfully happy following the herd around as they grazed. They seemed to instinctively trust the boy's quiet and gentle nature. Sometimes he sat on a rock and used his staff to create sketches in the sand while the animals mingled nearby. Other times he would close his eyes and listen to the birds, whose cheerful songs would bring a smile to his face and a new little tune to hum throughout the day. Had he been born into a wealthy family, Jophar would have followed his dream to paint and draw and even perhaps dabble with music. The arts were a fundamental part of his being, even out here with only the scrawny creatures to appreciate his work. With his eyes, ears, and heart he valued the beauty that surrounded him each day. He believed that his Lord was an artist and a musician as well. After selecting a safe spot for the animals to sleep each night, Jophar would lie down in their midst and admire the wonder of the stars in the sky. Confident that his Lord was watching over him, he would tap out a soothing melody that would gradually put both the animals and himself to sleep.

His father Nasir was the caretaker for the farm of a very wealthy landowner who appreciated and valued Nasir for the honourable man he was. It had been noted by several other landowners in the nearby towns that Nasir was not only conscientious at taking care of the needs of the farm, but he was also a devoutly religious man. And he was raising his sons to be the same, by training them in the ways of a God-fearing believer. As he considered Nasir a man of great wisdom, his master frequently asked for advice on local affairs when a trip to Jerusalem to ask advice from the Pharisees was deemed unnecessary. Nasir would take Jophar with him when he met with the other men, not trusting the older boys to watch out for their little brother's best interests when he was away. Even Jophar's disfigurement couldn't hide the fact that he was his father's son, for young Jophar unfailingly exhibited the same calm and wise judgment. On their way home, father and son often chatted about the events or articles that had been key to the discussions.

Sun-Lin

Sun-Lin had always avoided spending a lot of time with his grandfather. He had no patience for his grandfather's habit of pausing, mid-sentence, to sip at his tea, as if unsure how to continue speaking. Sun-Lin was positive he would find his elderly travelling companion just as boring as his classes had been. The trip certainly provided many hours for the two of them to talk, and surprisingly, Sun-Lin gradually found himself looking forward to their conversations. Each night, after settling into camp, the two had gone into their tent. Then, speaking in confidence, Ming had quietly shared his knowledge and the importance of the role they were playing in the history of the Persian Empire. Studying the stars and the maps they had brought along with them, Sun had discovered a fascination for learning that he had previously thought impossible.

They had been travelling for many days, first by elephant through lush jungles and now by camel over the desert sands. Rising before dawn they would travel until the sun was so high that the heat was almost unbearable and the star was nearly invisible in the bright blue sky. They would rest until the afternoon, when the animals had recovered enough to manage the trek. They only stopped when the evening darkness had settled in and travelling became too dangerous in their hastened journey to reach the foreign land to the northwest. Sun-Lin had his first glimpse of the sea at the shores of the Indian Ocean before heading north to follow the coast of the Persian Gulf. He wished they had time to make the trip slowly so he could explore and learn more about the new territories they travelled, but he had to content himself with the tales of adventure and conquest shared by the other men. Unsure how long their guiding star would remain visible, Ming pushed their caravan to travel as far as possible each day. Naturally, he was under great duress when he became so sick that he could no longer travel. The group had been forced to maintain camp for three days as they waited for Ming to regain enough strength to continue their journey. While still gravely ill, Ming whispered to Sun-Lin to delay no longer. Time was of the essence, and so he advised his grandson to stay focused on their duty. He must lead the men.

Only now, as Sun-Lin scanned the assembly of men before him, did he understand the risk that each of them had undertaken and the trust they had put into his grandfather's leadership. Failure was not an option. While each of them had great skills, they had relied on his grandfather as the leader to provide the guidance and information they required for fulfilling their roles. Grandfather's health was paramount to the success of the trip. Either the dread of losing his grandfather after they had finally formed such a close bond, or the fear that they would be lost without him, had Sun-Lin's stomach doing somersaults. Taking a deep breath, Sun-Lin knew that Grandfather must have had some secret concerns of his own. He realized that Grandfather had been subtly preparing him for this possibility from the very hour of the trip's conception. The knowledge he had passed on to Sun-Lin was now the means for everyone's success.

Sun-Lin squeezed his eyes tight and summoned the courage to take his grandfather's place as leader of the group of men before him. Would they listen to him and follow his orders? Their doubt in him, a mere child in their eyes, would have been well-founded. Chosen by his grandfather, tremendous thought had gone into the selection of these men. But they were not the only ones who had been selected for a purpose. Grandfather had chosen him as well. Confident these men would remain loyal and not let him down, Sun-Lin accepted his new role. While he had begun this trip a boy, the passing months and the enormous responsibility of their quest had matured him along the way. This was no longer a simple trip to escape the boredom of home, for he now knew that he had been handpicked. Now, with his grandfather still weak and unsteady cradled in his arms, he stepped up with confidence and conviction. He would see this mission through.

Tariq

Tariq bustled through the busy streets, barking orders to the two men that followed behind. They must hurry, as he feared they had taken far too long to reach their destination. Even a seasoned traveller like himself had been unprepared for the difficulties that they had encountered along their way. While a trek over the mountains to the north and then over the vast desert was surely formidable, their secondary route along the coastline to the mouth of the Red Sea should have been the swiftest and simplest leg of the journey. Instead, with bad weather and poor winds they had soon fallen behind his optimistic timetable. Then the boat had suffered hull damage when they took refuge at a simple port during a freak fall storm. Waiting for repairs to be completed had Tariq clutching at what was left of his worn patience. His initial wonder that this God who appeared to control even the stars had selected him for such an honourable and important role had faded with the appearance of sequential stumbling blocks. While his commitment to the counsel still pushed him to reach their destination, his doubt in an all-controlling God had grown daily.

They had all been relieved to finally reach land on the south-east coast of the Arabian Peninsula. Tariq had hoped that making record time would have allowed him the opportunity to visit the locations that he had read about in his studies about the people whom this Almighty God had long-declared to be His own. He would have very much liked to visit the sacred cave where Moses first received direction from his Lord in the burning bush for the release of the Hebrews held captive in Egypt, and Mt. Sinai where he had later been given the Ten Commandments. But time was of the essence and Tariq could not afford any more delays.

Weaving their way north through the mountain valleys, the caravan route they followed had become a frightening and chaotic journey. Travelled by many as the spice route to the north, the steep gorges created a natural pathway winding its way slowly inland and northward. Secretly armed beyond measure, he hoped to avoid catching the attention of the unruly bandits that preyed on the unprepared traveller. He knew that word would travel faster than his band of men if they were once discovered to be anything more than common traders. Hiding in the hillsides as the looters ran through the canyons, they had spent as many days taking cover as covering ground.

He had never had any patience for those that dealt harm to others and would have gladly stopped and passed judgment on the crooks. Yet the true purpose of his expedition outweighed his desire to bring these lowlifes to justice. Instead, on the occasions that they were detected, he had bribed and persuaded each of the corrupt thieves to let them pass unharmed. Tariq knew that such bribery only added to the bandits' purses and encouraged them to continue in their immoral behaviour. The irony was not lost on Tariq.

Elam

Elam knew he should seriously consider the recommendations and opinions of his advisors. His desire to become a great leader was so intense that he had only chosen advisors from a select list of men who had served other great leaders. To Elam, their previous positions were just as important as their intelligence and great capacity in the areas they oversaw. Their direction had always been accurate. They fulfilled their duties with the utmost care and diligence, and Elam appreciated their loyalty and skill equally.

Narod, his chief astronomer, had been with him since his first posting. Many months ago, Narod had come to him with news about a dazzling new star gleaming in the night sky. The appearance of this astounding new star heralded stories of the Jew's Messiah. Elam had taken genuine pleasure following along while Narod thoroughly examined the historical story. As their leader, it would be wise to be mindful of what the people of the land believed. Elam had hoped that government officials would request an inquiry be made regarding the star, but they had stayed silent. Secretly he imagined himself locating this King of all Kings. To accompany such a group would have given sufficient validity to the purpose of his trip, but to head off on a wild tangent like this on his own could be the very undoing of everything he had worked so hard for. But what if this very star were as important as it appeared to be? Discovering this imminent royalty could be the critical moment that could put his name in the history books forever.

Elam could get no rest. In his study he had been pacing at all hours of the day and night, to the point where he had worn a path in the carpet. He knew that he must always be confident and strong in order to maintain the admiration and allegiance of the government officials. If he appeared foolhardy and reckless, there was no doubt that he would be relieved of his duties.

But Narod, who had worked in his employ for many years, had never led him astray. And now, the whole story was just so preposterous that Elam had to credit it as just too much to dream up. No doubt there was some thread of truth to it. Woven into what appeared to be a bygone bunch of drama and nonsense could be a prophecy above all others. Why had the religious leaders not made any moves to reveal this great moment? They had not even come to him asking for contributions for a gift to honour this new King. Finally acknowledging that he would probably never sleep until he sought the truth, Elam instructed Narod to covertly prepare for the trip.

Departing after the harvest meant delaying their trip by another few months, but Elam was positive the new irrigation system would ensure a considerable crop yield. It would therefore be prudent for him to risk his leadership on the heels of this certain success. He gathered together a sizable offering of costly frankincense and myrrh and prepared to head south in the direction of the star. He would have to travel quickly, for his period of indecision had unfortunately consumed what may have been very precious time. The star, while still significantly brighter than the others, had been dimming each day since it had first appeared. Who knew how much longer he had to locate this Messiah?

He chose two of his most dependable servants and, with Narod at his side, atop his best camels they set off. Elam considered it fortunate that due to Caesar's call for a census the well-worn roads quickened and eased their excursion. The cool winter nights made travel less appealing for most, so they shared the roads with only a few lone travellers. Those they met they left behind quickly, as they rode south towards their goal. Elam had been in the King of Judea's presence once before, several years prior, and he decided to try and avoid any meetings with Herod on this trip. He did not want to deal with the sinister man if he could avoid it. Trying to explain his appearance could be tricky and embarrassing. He knew he did not want to share with Herod the true reason for his trip. If he was lucky he would only appear to be unfit for his position, but if Herod thought that Elam was trying to supersede his authority, Elam knew he would not survive the confrontation.

Wanting to appear in all his regalia should he indeed find this new King, Elam dressed in his finery and then covered that with a long cloak of camel's hair. If this was indeed the Messiah, he would not be the only one there to pay Him tribute. The cumbersome combination made a poor choice for travelling but was an inconvenience he would gladly accept in order to look his best on this historical occasion. For the moment, the cloak allowed him to blend in with the others easily. He hoped to locate the baby, if there was one, quickly and quietly. Otherwise he would return home and no one would be the wiser for his dabbling into the folklore of archaic people.

Mary

Mary's mother grew increasingly concerned with each passing day. Mary had been perhaps just a little too eager at the onset of her betrothal to Joseph, and so she had advised her daughter that it was improper to be so openly excited. Then, like a fire drowned by a bucket of water, Mary had grown intensely quiet. She had lost her appetite. She had been distraught and depressed one moment, only to be overcome with joy the next. Mary was not handling her betrothal well, even though Joseph was an excellent choice for a husband. Mary's erratic behaviour was quite unacceptable and so she had been keeping her daughter hidden at home. She had hoped that Mary would soon come to her senses, but time was running out. The months of the betrothal were passing.

Mary had kept quiet over the angel's visit. Was it real? Was she going mad? While an inner peace seemed to wash over her as she rose each morning, by evening the daily activities took their toll and doubt seeped into her mind. As her body began to show the signs that her pregnancy was in fact real, she realized she could delay no longer. She must gather the courage to share her story with her parents. Unsure how she would convince them she was speaking the truth about the angel's visit and God's incredible blessing, she had been dreading the conversation. One morning, after her sister had been sent to the town well for their daily water, Mary had ushered her parents inside for a private discussion. Trying to assemble her thoughts, she had begun speaking softly. At first her words were only a whisper that her parents had to strain and lean in closely to hear. Then, gathering her courage, her voice had risen as she shared the amazing news with her parents. When the reality of her words sank in, Mary's father had become totally outraged. Jumping to his feet, he prepared to march over to Joseph's family home. He would force the boy to immediately comply with his marital obligations after his apparent weakness. Clutching at his arm to restrain him, Mary repeatedly declared Joseph was not the father. Swearing she had lain with no man and explaining the visit from the angel once again, she'd broken down into deep sobs and professed her innocence. Her father had turned silent. Dropping to the floor, he sat motionless, his head hung into his hands. Mary had looked to her mother for consolation, only to find her silently weeping, her head bobbing up and down, as she clasped and unclasped her hands in her lap.

Her father's cruel ranting had been so painful that it brought tears to Mary's eyes as she recalled the incident. When he had eventually run out of energy and slumped into silence, she had been sure he was deliberating over the form of her punishment. Perhaps he had considered abandoning her completely. Finally, after what had seemed liked hours, he looked up. Taking a deep breath, he apologized for his outburst. Taking her hands in his, he looked heavenward, closed his eyes, and prayed to their God. Acknowledging all of the Lord's blessings and asking for wisdom and discernment he sat quietly for a time. Then, in a soft, low voice, he asked Mary to repeat her story - leaving no detail out. Thinking back, she realized that shock had caused her father to act as he had. That he came to his senses so quickly was a testament to his wisdom and faith.

Mary's father no longer disbelieved, though he realized the danger brought by the truth. That this could be the ruin of their family was just the beginning. Mary would be lucky to be left with her life once the news got out. There was no way they would be able to convince the town of her innocence, and the punishment for blasphemy and adultery would be on everyone's lips. While her mother had sat weeping quietly throughout the entire ordeal, suddenly she spoke up. She had come up with a plan. Whispering "Elizabeth" to her husband, she rose and wordlessly gathered together some food and travelling supplies along with Mary's few personal possessions. Wrapping these items into a travel satchel, she pressed the bag into Mary's arms. Hugging her daughter close, she kissed her cheeks while tears ran down her own. Then she stepped back and pushed her out the door with her father. They left the next moment, with no farewells to her sister or friends. Mary just slipped out of sight as her father rushed them down a back street and out onto the road that would lead them to her aunt's home out in the country. Hidden away from prying eyes and nosey neighbours, Mary would stay there until her baby was born. That Elizabeth herself was with child only made it easier, as it would appear to others that Mary was simply going to assist her elderly relative with her pregnancy. No one would guess she was hiding her own. Her father would deal with Joseph and his family when he returned.

JOSEPH

JOSEPH considered himself to be a strong and fit individual, but the journey to Bethlehem had proven arduous even for him. That Mary followed along quietly each day without a single complaint spoke more of her character than words ever could, and Joseph felt his irritation rise again. Her stoic behaviour only seemed to emphasize his own selfishness, although the only ones to bear witness were the two of them. Why this bothered him was even more perplexing. It was her fault they were in this mess, and he really didn't care what she thought of him. And yet, somehow, he did. Each time he glanced her direction, she would offer a gentle smile. As if to defend himself he would scowl in return, only to see a look of pain drift across her eyes. The corners of her mouth would droop momentarily before resuming their look of quiet and soulful determination once again. Who would have thought that this gentle girl would possess such perseverance? Thinking back to his mother's reason for selecting Mary to be Joseph's wife brought a little chuckle to his lips. Joseph knew that under different circumstances he would have grown quite devoted to this strong young woman.

He kicked his sandal into the ground in annoyance, only to be enveloped in a cloud of dust. Coughing, he spat out the mouthful of grit that had filled his mouth with a swipe of his hand over his dust-covered face. One look at Mary told him that she too was cloaked in the fine powder that rose up from the road as they made their way towards Bethlehem. Not accustomed to so many travellers, the pathways had quickly become well-worn as the population travelled from every corner of the state to fulfil the census decreed by the Romans. The usually hard-packed surface had been loosened by a multitude of feet into a trail of dust. Billowing in the late fall winds it blanketed the groups as they migrated across the Judean countryside.

Ever since he had given into the dream and shared his vision with his mother, things had deteriorated. Joseph's meeting with Mary's father had been a disaster. Instead of exhibiting respect to his future father-in-law, he had lost his temper and behaved like a spoiled and immature little boy. Yelling and screaming at the man, he demanded Mary's father bring her to fulfill her vows. Tight-lipped,

Mary's father had refused to cooperate. Yet Joseph had persisted. His family expected him to stand up to his responsibilities, and Mary had better accept hers. It wasn't until Joseph shared his dream about the angel that Mary's father relented and finally revealed the truth about Mary's pregnancy and her hiding place. With his dream validated, Joseph's bold confidence withered. The frightening course his life had taken took hold of him. Mary's father questioned Joseph's plans. Struggling to resist the urge to run from the situation, Joseph couldn't bring himself to offer reassurance to Mary's father. Nothing was working out the way he had thought it would and he had given up trying.

His delay in collecting Mary meant that they had been forced to travel with the last of the journeyers, and the groups that would come up from behind and pass them through the day became less frequent as the days went by. Knowing that there was safety in their numbers, Joseph prayed they would make it to Bethlehem unharmed. Even with Mary's condition slowing them considerably, they managed to find a group to camp with each night. Mary was weary and completely drained, and so they would take long breaks when the midday sun was at its hottest to make the journey more manageable for both her - and for Zechariah's old donkey. Months back the old man had visited his father's workshop. Joseph remembered the crazy antics and public display Zechariah had performed while appearing to be mute. In contrast, this time it had been impossible to get Zechariah to stop jabbering. Eventually he had relented to Zechariah's persuasion and accepted the old beast for their trip, if only to calm him. But now he was thankful for the reliable animal, and for the extra supplies.

Joseph had been unconscious of the passage of time when he had finally made his way out to the elderly couple's home to unite with Mary, and so he hadn't been prepared to find Elizabeth nursing her new son and Mary heavily pregnant. Unbeknownst to Caesar, his directive that everyone must return to the city of his forefather had provided the perfect plan for Joseph. He had been relieved not to have to return home, as Mary's condition would have meant immediate accusations. Yet his procrastination meant that the trip was far more difficult than it could have been.

Shaking his head in frustration Joseph examined his present predicament. Look at him dragging an old donkey, his betrothed pregnant with a child not his own, through a town too full of people to accommodate them. What had he been thinking?

Bethlehem was bursting at the seams. The census had meant that the town was straining with all the displaced people crammed into the streets. Tempers ran high as frustrations led to anger and violence. The street noise was nearly deafening as people yelled and animals bayed, barked, and ducked between the people. The alleys had become temporary homes for many as they satisfied the census requirements and tried to procure the necessities they needed for their journey home. Bethlehem, unaccustomed to so many travellers, had quickly run out of supplies. The little that was left was priced beyond belief. Joseph knew that his father would also be required to register as the head of his household and could be here somewhere, but in this crowd, it was impossible to locate him. As much as he desired the security that being with him offered, not finding him was probably for the best. For how could he have explained his predicament when even he couldn't believe it himself? There was nothing good to come from finding him, so he prayed that they never crossed paths here in Bethlehem.

Visibly distressed, the fear in Mary's eyes screamed out to Joseph. He had to find a place for her to rest. Struggling to move down the street without jostling Mary, who clung to the donkey's neck while she wobbled her way beside him, Joseph pleaded with and begged every merchant and innkeeper for even a corner of their shop. He had to get them off the street. He was completely beside himself. At a small inn on the edge of town, the innkeeper's wife, who had been standing behind her husband during Joseph's plea for a room, saw Mary's condition and took pity on them. She suggested they might stay in the stable at the back where they kept their few livestock. Joseph understood that this was probably the best they would find, and so he led his wife to the stable. His pride may have suffered more had Mary expressed any qualms about their crude accommodation, but she was in such a state that she didn't seem to even register where she was. Giving in to her exhaustion, she had lain down amongst the hay with a young calf, and there among the farm animals, without fanfare or flourish, Mary had given birth to a son, the Lamb of God.

Gabriel

EVER since his role with the last delegation of angels when he had told Mary of her pregnancy and then told Joseph to fulfil his vows, Gabriel had been waiting anxiously for a cue from the Lord. The Heavenly Father had shared His plan with the hosts of angels and allowed them to rejoice as they waited patiently for the miracle to unfold before them.

Now it was time. The Lord took Gabriel and indicated the small shepherd boy to whom Gabriel would make his glorious announcement. Gabriel was confused. The little fellow couldn't possibly be the one he was to boldly proclaim the birth of the Lord to. Gabriel was missing something. He questioned the Lord, who assured him that Jophar was definitely the correct recipient. How would the world ever learn that He was the Father to each and every one of them unless Gabriel broke the glorious news to one whom the people of the Earth had deemed unworthy? No great amount of knowledge or wealth. No rituals and ceremonies. None were required. God's children had to know that this was not a gift for only a few, but for all. To believe was the only requirement, and faith, the Lord had assured Gabriel, Jophar had in full measure.

The young boy had listened intently to his earthly father as he shared the great news of a coming Messiah. In the same way that he celebrated his freedom during the Passover, Jophar's confidence in God's love for him gave him reason to be thankful. Even with all the suffering he had endured, the young boy would not need validation from the Earth and her inhabitants, and the Lord was confident that the simple, solid faith in the pint-sized child would stand up to the test.

Unable to contain his eagerness, and with God's note of assurance, Gabriel swooped down over the boy. Rising up to his full measure to be sure to impress the young lad, Gabriel declared the wonderful news of the newborn King.

Gabriel waited to see his declaration get the boy's attention. Would he seize the importance of what he was being told? Initially the boy had appeared terrified, and, for more than a few minutes, dazed by the entire experience. Gabriel had wondered if perhaps the Lord would want him to find another more suitable recipient, but just as he began to recede from the child to join the others in praise, the boy had jumped up with an energy and excitement that just might have surpassed Gabriel's own. He began sprinting for town. Thrilled with the result and his task complete, Gabriel retreated to the heavens to watch as the Earth received her King.

Jophar

As the sun set and dusk turned to night, Jophar began his evening ritual. Hanging around his neck was the little drum that his father had fashioned for him years ago when his older brothers had begun whistling around the house. Jophar's deformed mouth made it impossible to achieve such a sound. This gift from his father was one of his most prized possessions, and had he been rich, he would have traded his gold or a female camel ready to birth for it. Now, he tapped out a pleasant little rhythm that brought the sheep and goats scampering towards him. In the crook of his arm, carefully cuddled against the evening cold, was the little lamb that had been born just a few days earlier. Tragically, it had been born blind and was immediately abandoned by its mother. Jophar had ensured that it was nursed with one of the other little lambs and had carried it about with a paternal love. Like him, it was different from the others, but he knew that he had a purpose, and so did this little lamb.

He had just settled in for the night when suddenly the sky became so brightly illuminated he had to shield his eyes from the glare. Terrified, he had jumped up to gather the animals and head for the farm when an angel appeared before him. Ablaze in glowing light, the angel reached out to Jophar. He froze in fear.

"Jophar," the angel said, "tonight, a baby has been born in a stable in Bethlehem. The Son of God, He will be called the King of Kings. Go, follow the star, and see for yourself."

Breaking out into a dash and running back to town as fast as his feet would carry him, he couldn't believe that he was part of this miracle. Him, the poor disfigured shepherd boy, had been visited by an angel on high. The angel had held out his hand to him. Thousands upon thousands of angels had gathered behind the first to sing praises to the Lord. Brighter than daylight, the sky had been full of them. Was he hallucinating? Had he lost his senses? The angel assured him he had not.

Now it was dark again except for the dazzling star that appeared almost directly in front and above him on the very edge of town. Caught between the desire to see the babe for himself and to run to his father and share the great news, Jophar had decided to confirm the location of the baby Messiah before finding his father. Rushing up to the stable, Jophar burst in on the little family. Joseph roughly pulled him back out of the shelter of the stalls, demanding an explanation for his behaviour. Between gulps for air, Jophar had told Joseph about the angel and his message. Had he found the right place? Was this the baby Messiah? Jophar's inquiry seemed to cause Joseph serious distress as he clasped his chest and struggled to breathe. Concerned that he had been misguided in his decision to seek out the babe, Jophar was about to go to his father at home when Joseph recovered. Then, holding a finger to his lips to make certain Jophar would be quiet, Joseph stepped aside and let him inside the enclosure.

Could this really be the Saviour that his father had taught him about? Was this the Redeemer for all of humanity? Jophar quietly stepped inside the small stable and knelt down between the sleeping animals. The baby lay in a pile of soft hay only a few feet in front of him. A glow, like that of the angels, seemed to hover around the infant and Jophar felt a great peace wash over him. A cool breeze blew past as the baby's father appeared behind him. With a tenderness earned by much suffering, he gently laid the little lamb still tucked under his arm next to the baby. The little lamb would provide warmth. Jophar recalled the prophecies taught to him by his father. He knew that one day this baby would suffer more than he could ever imagine so that he could be reunited with The Almighty. Silently, reverently, and with a wisdom found only in the very aged, Jophar acknowledged this was his Saviour.

JOSEPH

JOSEPH stumbled out of the stable. Stunned by the magnitude of what he was only just beginning to grasp he dropped to his knees, his hands grabbed at the sand, and he shook his head. Up to this very moment he had never truly believed that the baby Mary carried was the Messiah. Deep down he had been harbouring so much anger at God for asking him to take on such a task as caring for a woman that was obviously not worthy of any husband. He was sacrificing his future. And yet, just moments before, the shepherd boy had stood before him, panting from lack of breath and visibly fatigued from rushing to see if what the angel had told him was true.

"Have I found the newborn King?" the young lad had gasped between ragged breaths. Overwhelmed with guilt and shame, tears of remorse shook Joseph to the core of his being. How he wished he had been more faithful. Looking up to the heavens, he begged God to forgive him.

How could he have been so blind and narrow-minded? God had selected him to be incredibly blessed, yet he had been snubbing it all this time. He thought back to how his mother had forced him to obey the dream. They had been more concerned about their reputation than the will of God. What a failure he had been in supporting Mary through this ordeal. What would the townspeople think when they saw how he had failed to provide for her and the baby? The Messiah, in a stable! Joseph shook his head again as he realized the depth of his grief.

Looking back over the events that had passed, Joseph finally saw God's hand in them all. His trip to Zechariah and Elizabeth's to fetch Mary and bring her home as his wife would have resulted in horrific consequences. Caesar calling the census had been a gift in disguise. Packing up the donkey and setting out for Bethlehem, God had presented the perfect excuse for their departure and provided for them each step of the way. Joseph had realized as they made their way towards Bethlehem that there was nothing for them at home and to return lacked wise judgment. Now, convincing his family of the truth would be just as impossible. He hadn't believed it himself, even after the countless dreams telling him otherwise. Mary would be viewed as a disgrace to her family and could be held accountable for her apparent actions. Joseph acknowledged he simply didn't have a strong enough faith to deal with it. He was already exhausted just thinking about the failure that would come with trying to get the people to believe. It was just that much easier for them to stay here. Thankfully his father had taught him well, and he seemed to have a natural talent for working with wood. Reading the grain, gauging its strength and flexibility, he had already proven himself to be a skilled carpenter. He would try to find work in Bethlehem. With all the extra people, the city was straining to meet all their demands. As he stepped back into their lowly temporary home, he couldn't stop the tears from pouring down his face. He had provided a dirty manger as the place for the birth of the Son of God. What had he done?

And then he noticed the little shepherd boy, kneeling in front of Mary and Jesus. Oblivious to the surroundings, his face radiated pure joy. His faith was palpable. And then suddenly Joseph understood. Acknowledging the huge responsibility and vowing to rise to the challenge, Joseph allowed the joy of what was taking place to fill his heart. God had reunited with his people.

Mary

One glance at Joseph as he stepped into the humble stable told Mary that he finally understood. The tears coursing down his face while he looked from her, to the baby, to the shepherd boy, and then the ground said more than words ever would. Her world had been turned upside down when the angel had appeared to her nine months ago. Overwhelmed by the confusing emotions that tore through her, she had thought that Joseph would be her one source of support during this test of her faith. Simply speechless as she was overcome with the joy of being chosen to be the mother of the Son of God, and then immediately crushed by the ramifications her pregnancy would have on her and her future with Joseph, she had prayed that her new husband would be strong in character and in faith in God. Mary had felt safe and secure at Zechariah and Elizabeth's, for they had opened their hearts and their home to her. They had been pillars to strengthen her faith. When Joseph had arrived and shared his dream, announcing that he was there to take her as his wife and that they were leaving to comply with Caesar's decree, she was positive that he had felt God's hand as powerfully as herself. She had given up on her dream of growing old with Joseph, and so his news that he wanted to uphold his part in their marriage had Mary overcome with awe in what was surely the influence of her Lord. Joseph believed. Why else would he sacrifice his future for her? When she had spoken of the angel appearing to her regarding the coming baby, she thought Joseph had understood. And yet it became clear as they made their way to Bethlehem that Joseph did not share her faith nor her peace surrounding their predicament. He was acting out of something far more self-serving it seemed, although what, she couldn't understand. It was as if by doing this he had thought he was better than everyone else, sacrificing his entire future to care for a pregnant, unwed, young woman. Now, looking at Joseph as he struggled with his shame, Mary felt her confidence in him return. Slowly he stepped around the small shepherd boy and crouched down beside her. Taking his cloak from his shoulders he draped it around Mary, and reaching out tenderly, he let the infant grasp his little finger with his hand. Finally, Joseph would be her husband.

Nasir

Nasir had been horrified when Jophar came running from the fields in the middle of the night. Was there danger, a wolf perhaps? Why had he left the animals unattended? Jophar had staggered in breathless and desperate to share the good news. He had spent a few moments with the little baby sleeping quietly in front of him before jumping up and racing home to his father. Winded from his exertion, he began sharing his incredible story between gulps for air. Jophar had never before been so irresponsible with the animals. Concerned for their safety, Nasir had grabbed the boy by the arm and pulled him along while they ran back to the hills. Relieved to find the animals still safe, he took a deep breath to regain his composure and then sat down among them. With Jophar securely by his side, his arm around him, he let the coolness settle over them. He finally listened to his son's amazing story. The Lord had returned. Now, with great excitement flowing through him, he was desperate for dawn so they could return the animals to the farm and he could go see the baby for himself.

It was midday when Nasir left Joseph, Mary, and the baby Jesus at the stable, his mind perplexed and emotions torn. How could the Lord of all be a little baby to this peasant couple? As a devout Jew, if this were truly the Messiah, he would be most honoured to be a part of revealing Him to the world. With no scrolls to study, he tried hard to remember all the stories that his father had shared with him so long ago. He tried to piece the events together.

Knowing the little family would want to travel to Jerusalem to dedicate their new son to God, he offered to assist them with his mules and cart. He would be patient and wait until the Pharisees concurred with his son's story. Until then, Nasir had to keep Jophar quiet for the boy's own safety. He warned his son to keep the baby's location secret. With all the strangers and undesirable activities that had arrived in Bethlehem thanks to Caesar's census, it would be very dangerous for the young family if word of the miracle was shared with the wrong people. Fully aware of the evil that lurked inside of man, the baby's safety would keep Jophar from repeating his story. They would be able to watch and see if the baby turned out to be the great King without telling anyone else. Returning to their daily chores and duties, Jophar would visit the baby boy every day, content to watch him grow and make him laugh.

Mary recovered and Joseph began working for Nasir in the stables. Jophar was to direct anyone inquiring on the baby Jesus or a new king to his father. Nasir would advise Joseph and let him decide on the plan of action. Jophar did his best to put the event out of his mind, but still awestruck, he would talk with his father about the great miracle. They agreed to continue to wait and watch. So far no one had shown any interest in locating or worshipping the little baby.

When the time came for Jesus to be dedicated, Nasir kept his word. Packing the cart with Mary, Jesus, Jophar, and the two doves to sacrifice for Jesus' dedication, they had headed west to Jerusalem and the great temple. As soon as Nasir had spied the city gates in the distance, he pulled Jophar from the cart. Quickly arranging with Joseph to meet outside the temple, Nasir and Jophar had rushed off ahead of them. Nasir had met with the Pharisees on several occasions in the past and he hoped they would appreciate the urgency in his request and grant him a meeting. After describing the situation to the Pharisees, Nasir was very disappointed when they had taken one look at Jophar and laughed. What kind of man would take the word of a disfigured and dimwitted young boy? This type of response was not new to Jophar and his father, but Nasir had thought the Pharisees would be above this cruel and absurd behaviour. Nasir had considered bringing Joseph and Jesus with him directly to the meeting, but when the Pharisees didn't even want to hear about the angels or the baby in the stable, he was happy he had not. In fact, the Pharisees did not appear to be particularly interested in the Messiah's return at all. Instead they kept busy fulfilling the sacrifices and accepting tributes to the Roman government, all the while standing in the grand doorway of the temple for everyone to admire.

Nasir found the Pharisees' pompous attitude troubling. Wouldn't it be wise to review the prophecies? As his trust in the Pharisees wavered, doubt of what he had thought to be true began to creep into his mind. That the Messiah had been born to this simple man and woman seemed harder to believe as each day passed. Somehow, he had to confirm the Messiah's earthly parentage.

Abandoning the idea that he would find validation at the temple, Nasir and Jophar had retreated from the temple stairs. Disappointed, they searched among the many in the courtyard for Joseph and Mary. After spotting them just entering the temple courtyard, Nasir, gathering up Jophar, prepared to join them. They had just reached the little group when a fiery old man forcibly pushed his way through the crowds and rushed up to Joseph and Mary. Nasir recognized him as the man who had caught his eye when he had arrived at the temple gates earlier. His weathered face had looked particularly anxious and had peered at Nasir and his son with intense curiosity. He wondered if the old man recognized them from a previous trip, even though he couldn't recall having met the fellow before.

Joseph was about to push past the old man when he stunned them all, whispering, "I know who this baby is." Turning towards Mary and solemnly laying his hands on the infant in her arms, the elderly fellow raised his face heavenwards and murmured his thankfulness to the Lord. Then, slowly and reverently, he returned his attention to the small group. Taking them in with his gaze, he divulged God's promise that he would see the Messiah with his own eyes. He had been waiting a very long time. Praying in the temple courtyard by day and sleeping by the temple gates each night, he had watched vigilantly for many years. On more than one occasion he had lost hope, only to have God encourage him to hold on a little longer. Today, God had fulfilled His promise. Then, gently taking the child into his gnarled and wrinkled hands, he lifted the baby Jesus high above him. Proclaiming his faith in a strong and powerful voice, he urged everyone close by to stop and listen.

"Here is the Messiah; I have seen him with my own eyes. Our salvation has come!" Many of the passersby stopped and stared. Was the man so far gone in years that he had lost his mind? Nasir could see that the old man's bellowing had gotten the Pharisees' attention as well, and they looked especially disturbed. Joseph and Mary didn't know what to do. Dazed by the outlandish man's bold declaration, they had stood silently, too stunned to speak. Chatter broke out amongst the crowd when a woman, appearing just as aged as the man, slipped through the others. Dropping to her knees, she repeated the announcement and gave thanks to God. The people in the courtyard gathered to watch and listen. Whoever these elderly people were, they were obviously known to the crowd as faithful followers of God. In fact, their announcements seemed to have astonished everyone. Nasir gathered that they didn't make a habit of shouting out wild statements that folks would disregard and ignore. Instead, the group looked inquisitive, offering credibility to their proclamations. Nasir felt his conviction return. Finally, they had received a sign from God. He waited for the Pharisees to approach but they seemed resolute, refusing to acknowledge the statements with their presence.

It took several hours before they had finally been able to leave the temple. Surrounded, questions had flown about as the mass of people tried to ascertain Jesus' heritage from Simeon, the devout old man who had first recognized the baby as the Messiah. Nasir had expected the crowd to follow them when they left, but was surprised when the folks had stayed behind with Simeon and Anna. Simeon had sat down on the ground and offered thanks to God while the people plied him with questions. Unprepared to accept the truth, their doubt kept them from the simple joy that Simeon and Jophar had displayed. Nasir saw himself in their behaviour and realized how blessed his son with his unquestioning faith really was.

Relishing in this validation of Jesus' birthright, Joseph had decided he would take his family home to Nazareth. He wanted to raise the boy in the security of his family home. With the corroboration of Simeon and Anna, he was sure any accusations of infidelity would be put to rest. Nasir was sorry they would be leaving Bethlehem, but he understood. They agreed that Joseph would take the cart and mules after returning Nasir and Jophar to Bethlehem. They would rest at the inn for a few days while Joseph sourced some supplies before setting off north to Galilee. Joseph was sure the news of Jesus' birth would reach his hometown before he did. He could feel his ego begin to swell inside and did a quick check. He would have to keep a tight rein on his pride.

Sun-Lin

HOPING to find favour with the present leader of the strange land, Grandfather had explained to Sun-Lin that they would probably be required to give some of the considerable amounts of gold and jewels they had brought with them to purchase a moment with the newborn King. Grandfather surmised that the current ruler may be reluctant to allow anyone else time with the one who would be the greatest ruler of all. Sun-Lin understood that it was now his responsibility to see that these treasures made it into the hands of the coming sovereign and that the Emperor's tribute be presented. Grandfather had disclosed the inferred location to Sun-Lin during one of their evening talks. Thankful for his sharp memory, he had swiftly gathered the righteous men together to propose a new plan. The star they had been following had been dimming each day. Hesitant to trust that it would remain visible for much longer, he directed the group to make inquiries on the location of the city of David. He hoped they would be able to head straight to the town where the new King would be, while recovering the time they had lost and avoiding any conflict with the present leader. Sun-Lin had his grandfather lifted up onto his own camel and he held him securely while he slept. The men loaded up the supplies. After arranging their own beasts around Sun-Lin in a protective manner, they drove forward.

Many days had passed when Sun-Lin had the party set up camp just outside of a little town; the star had taken on a new brilliance just a day ago and Sun took it as a sign that they were close to their destination. With two of the men along he would make subtle enquiries in the town about a baby's birth. He did not want to alert any outlaws to their purpose. As they made their way over the last little hill, Sun-Lin spotted a young shepherd boy tending a small flock of sheep. Judging that they would be safe revealing their quest to a humble shepherd, he urged his camel forward to join their translator and then together they approached the boy for assistance. Still cradling his grandfather in his arms when they drew near, Sun-Lin noticed that the boy was disfigured. He began to doubt the boy's ability to help as he had hoped.

Taking a chance, he queried, "Have you heard any news about a new King?" Sun-Lin mentioned that his grandfather was unwell and he feared the old man would not live long enough to have the honour of seeing their quest through to completion. He had not expected a response, and was astonished by the confidence and conviction that the shepherd boy radiated when he responded.

Tariq

THE star hovered just above him to his right. Tariq was so close now that he could barely contain his excitement. As he rushed back to the city gates where the rest of his men waited, he shook his head. He was utterly stunned at the ignorance of Herod. Positive that it would be faster to approach the present leader directly to obtain the exact location of the future King, Tariq had paid a tremendous sum for an immediate appointment with the local ruler. Imagine his surprise when the man appeared to have no knowledge of the great event taking place in his land. Instead, he asked Tariq to return and direct him after finding the baby so he too could honour the future King. Tariq wondered if the man had simply avoided exposing the whereabouts of the baby in order to retain the greatest favour with him.

The guiding star that had appeared to be dimming had reappeared with a new brilliance last night and Tariq was frantic. He had visited the markets to quickly restock and then pack up the camels before heading out in search this morning. He could not afford to waste time worrying about Herod now, and so he had allowed his servant Lamir to deal with the men that had begun following them when they had left the palace.

Tariq and his men had approached the little town with scepticism. Surely this couldn't be the place. No grand palaces or even homes built with great wealth were evident. In fact, apart from a significant farm just to the north, the city appeared to be home to only a modest population of pitiable income. And yet the star shone above it with an unmatched brilliance that couldn't be ignored. Looking for a safe place to take care of the animals, Tariq's men located the stables of the large farm that was under the care of Jophar's father Nasir. Nasir had greeted the men himself and questioned their purpose. When Tariq mentioned his search, Nasir had summoned Joseph, who was presently preparing the cart for his family's journey home, and together they probed Tariq with questions. Could he tell them how he came of this information? Did he have any specific details of what he was looking for? Tariq left little doubt of his sincerity in the two men's minds. He displayed great wisdom, with knowledge dating back to the time of King David and consequently the God that David had loved so much. Tariq explained the historical manuscripts documenting the star and its significance. He recounted his studies on the land and the people, of blessed birthright, who followed this mighty God. Had the Jews not been promised a Messiah? Finally, Tariq wanted to know if the Christ had come.

Jophar had brought the star to their attention when he had shared the angel's news, but Joseph was unaware of its importance. He did not know that it had reawakened in brilliance. That Tariq had used this star as a guide to lead his men from distant lands to their location seemed a great leap of faith. Originally suspicious of the strangers, Joseph realized that Tariq truly was a man seeking the Son of God. He agreed to take him to the baby Jesus. Joseph and Mary had moved into a room at the back of the inn now that most of the people that had crowded Bethlehem for the census had departed for home. Until their trip to Jerusalem, there had been no reason to leave and so Joseph had found work with Nasir building and repairing the tools for the farm to pay for his little family's keep while Mary had recovered and cared for the newborn baby Jesus.

Elam

APPROACHING the outskirts of a small town, Elam sent his servants to look for lodging. While the dismal-looking inn was a far cry from the extravagant accommodations he was accustomed to, he would have endured much worse to save himself the greater unease of possibly having the wicked magistrate, Herod, hear of his visit. Suspecting that the evil official could even have guards watching the Messiah, Elam was determined to stay as obscure as possible. Securing rooms at the little inn on the edge of town was a perfect disguise, as far as he was concerned. Hidden out of sight, they could seek out this baby King without attracting any notice.

Narod, however, was more than overjoyed. He was beside himself. If the star indicated the location of the Messiah, then they must be very near indeed. Preparing to ask the innkeeper's wife about any recent births, Narod nearly passed out from excitement when a young woman with her infant son walked past him and into the kitchen. Could it be? Were they exactly where they needed to be? How could they be sure that this was indeed the Messiah?

But when Narod shared his dilemma, Elam quickly flattened his advisor's enthusiasm. This was merely a coincidence. A king would be born into riches, a family with stature, and not unto this lowly woman. How could a boy learn what was expected and the values required to be a great king if he wasn't surrounded by the things that made men great? For Elam was well aware of the training required to be a great leader, and nothing here convinced him that these people had the means to provide any of it. Besides, if this was the baby, where were the crowds that would surely have come to honour him? They may be arriving late to the party, but certainly there should be some devout believers still here. One glance should have persuaded Narod that this was the truth, but he persisted - quite certain that they were in the very spot they wanted to be.

Standing on the town's border and looking down the main street, Elam was convinced of quite the opposite. Bethlehem was obviously nothing more than a village of meagre means. It had all the appearances of having had a great storm blow through. This was not the birthplace of a great king; he was convinced. They would stay the night and begin their journey home again in the morning. This wild-goose chase was over, as far as he was concerned.

Still in his camel's-hair cloak, Elam and his men took lodging at the little inn. They had just settled in after a good meal when Joseph and Nasir arrived with Tariq behind him. Tariq's stature was quite impressive, even as he stood quietly at the door, and his appearance hinted at a much more distinguished and learned man. Initially alarmed, Elam's first thought was that the stranger had come from Herod. Once he discovered the visitor was a foreigner like themselves, he invited him to join them. Was this man someone of importance? Should Elam reveal who he was? Did his posture suggest that he was an important man too?

HEROD

DEEPLY troubled, Herod considered his choices. Earlier that week several Pharisees had come to him to discuss an incident that had taken place at the temple. They had asked him what he wished to do about it. Clearly, they had found the event disturbing, and after reviewing some ancient prophecies felt that his leadership was threatened - although they would never have said this outright. Not wanting to appear alarmed, he had passed the whole affair off as being trivial while silently pondering how he could privately find out more about it. Then, just a few days later, a foreigner had paid a considerable sum to meet with him and inquire about the same occurrence. Again, he had shrugged off the questions, this time in the hopes of discouraging the visitor. Acting quickly, he had surreptitiously ordered two of his guards to follow the stranger's troupe and report back. Now, with the two fools dead at his feet for their disobedience, he was no further ahead. If their story was to be believed, and Herod did believe it, apparently a trusted servant of the man had been far shrewder than his own soldiers and had noticed the two men following them. Shadowing his master as they made their way to the city gates, the arrogant duo had obviously been useless at trying to blend in with the crowd at the market.

Creatively cunning, the clever protector had confronted his two men, playing up to them, implying he had no love for his master. After being dragged from his homeland and brought along on a crazy journey with a madman, whatever their purpose, perhaps he could be of some assistance. The guards had disclosed their intentions for following Tariq to locate the baby King for Herod. The wise sentinel had sized up the lazy men accurately and suggested they could exchange favours. He would go along and find out the information his new comrades required if they commended his actions to Herod on his return, possibly securing a position amongst them. The guards couldn't believe their good fortune and, falling for the trap, quickly agreed, eager to revel on the corrupt side of town while waiting for his return. Unfortunately for them, they were caught by one of Herod's advisors the next morning when they had stupidly brought their carousing behaviour onto the streets and to the attention of passersby. Herod's rage had been immediate, knowing that this opportunity to discover the whereabouts of the baby King had been lost. Secretly fearful, he had taken his fury out on the men. Stepping over their still bodies, he fumed at their ineptness. Now he would have to find another way to find and ultimately deal with this threat to his territory.

Jophar

HOME from Jerusalem, Jophar had returned to the hills with his little flock. Tapping away on his drum he had been blissfully happy. Though he would miss his visits with baby Jesus when Joseph and Mary left for Nazareth, he was as content as always. No one in Bethlehem knew of the event in Jerusalem, so they had returned to their quiet lives with no one showing any interest in Jesus. Jophar had found himself disappointed in people again. Mankind's salvation should have been marked with great rejoicing and reverent ceremony. Instead it was going virtually unnoticed. His father had assured him that God was in control. One day, all would be revealed.

He had noticed the troop of men when he had woken at dawn. Their tents and animals could be seen in the distance and their voices carried across the hillside to Jophar. It took only an instant for Jophar to wonder if these men sought out Jesus. Lacking the skepticism of the average man, Jophar was sure that at some point men would come searching for the little baby. Though he constantly asked his father if he had heard of any inquiries, his father would remind him that no one had shown any interest in finding Jesus. At least no one until now, and this was not a local inquiring about Jesus. These were foreigners, a boy similar in age to his older brothers and an elderly man that appeared to be weak and unwell. Jophar's inner caution told him to be wary, but the boy had shared an amazing story of great travels to search for a new King. The small group of men behind the two gave only hints at the exceptional individuals they must be, for they appeared humble and modest. And from the looks of the old man, his time would likely be short indeed. Jophar was positive it was no mistake that this group had found him out here in the hills. God had led them to him so he could lead them to the baby Jesus. Jophar felt his faith revived by the group's inquiry. Finally, people were taking an interest in the holy baby. Remembering his father's words of caution and unwilling to reveal Jesus and put him at risk, he was suddenly inspired. Used to having his intelligence questioned because of his cleft lip he chose to use it to his advantage. Boldly he insisted that he could help the travel party. They could take the sick grandfather to the inn on the edge of town to be cared for while the others looked into the matter of the King. They would have no idea that the baby at the inn was the King they searched for. Eager to visit the Christ child again, Jophar quickly secured his herd in a little pen and then led Sun-Lin and Ming-Tan into town.

Jophar had planned on settling the group at the inn and then going to find his father and Joseph. Instead he was surprised to find the Inn full, with his father and Joseph already gathered in the company of more foreigners. His wariness of people engulfed him and he instantly feared for the baby. What were they doing there?

Nasir spied Jophar at the door and rushed over to tell him about Tariq's and Elam's journeys to find the Christ child. There was no doubt in anyone's mind that Jophar had been incredibly blessed. Jophar had never been concerned about his reputation or being proven right. He had only wanted to share what he knew to be the truth: the great news of the Messiah. Finally, the word would be out. He would have been proud to take Sun-Lin and Ming-Tan right to Jesus, but he knew his place, and knowing it would be wrong not to, he introduced them to his father and Joseph. After explaining his meeting with Ming-Tan and Sun-Lin out in the hills and the expedition their troupe was on, he left them with the men and sought out the baby. Obscured by the large crowd of men, he found the little boy gurgling and laughing on his mother's lap in the corner of the room. Large sacks and chests had been placed on the floor around where Mary sat cradling the baby, and a stranger was bowed before Jesus in obvious worship. Jophar had never considered giving the baby gifts of adoration. He had fashioned a few toys from bits of wood with Joseph's guidance and had even let him play with his prized little drum, but not until now had the idea of honouring Jesus with gifts been a thought to consider. Jophar felt his confidence drain from him. He had been in the presence of God and had done nothing. His eyes filled with tears as he stepped back into the shadows in the corner of the room, too embarrassed to face anyone. Should he try to leave? At the same instant that he turned to run for the door, Jophar's father called out to him, "Come and meet the visitors. They wanted to meet the boy with whom God had chosen to share His amazing news." Still shaking from his humble revelation, Jophar dutifully joined his father.

"What have you done to deserve such a blessing?" the men had asked. They would have traded all their gold and stature for such an honour. Jophar had considered this question himself nearly every day as he tended to the sheep on the hills. Why had the angel appeared to him? There was no point in sharing his wonderful news with anyone. No one would believe him. So why? The answer had always eluded him, but here, in the presence of these wealthy and knowledgeable men, it suddenly became clear. God hadn't chosen him for his wealth. He didn't have to be smart or know that all the historical writings had come true. Instead, he had been chosen because he believed. It was his faith, free and available to everyone, that had put him there before the angel. God hadn't come to Earth to be given gifts. He had come as a gift to them.

Sun-Lin

Sun-Lin knew he should be paying closer attention, but he had grown weary trying to piece everything together. His grandfather had perked up following their arrival at the inn and the discovery of the baby, and he had sat up among the other foreign men. With the assistance of two of his aides, he was listening intently to the translator and animatedly adding to the conversation. Sun-Lin sat behind him, trying to make sense of everything he heard.

When he had been told at the onset of their trip that they were going in search of a baby that would be a future king, he had no difficulty understanding the idea. The son of the present emperor had only been born a few years ago at the palace, and Sun-Lin had seen him on many occasions. His nannies would often take him for walks in the palace gardens while the older boys were given their lessons there. One day the little boy would take his father's place, and the legacy would continue. And so, it wasn't until their arrival at the inn that Sun-Lin became confused. Yes, here was a baby. But where was his kingdom? There was no palace and no servants. Instead, there was quite the opposite.

Ming-Tan noticed the perplexed look on Sun-Lin's face. Drawing him closer into the group of men, Grandfather asked what was troubling him. Was he having difficulty understanding the translator? Sun-Lin was unsure whether to admit his confusion in front of these strangers, but his grandfather persisted. While Grandfather hoped to regain his health and survive the long trip home, Sun-Lin had been reminded that he must be prepared to take his place. Like the wise men before them who had ensured the accuracy of prophecies, Ming Tan and Sun-Lin now had the great responsibility to account for this event correctly.

"Speak up," Grandfather encouraged, "and let the men answer your questions." Sun-Lin knew his grandfather was right, and so he hesitantly spoke up.

"How would this little baby become a future King?" he asked. "Who would serve him? Where were his followers?"

All the men became quite solemn. Slowly Narod rose and walked around the group. Then, crouching down so he could look Sun-Lin in the eyes, Narod spoke slowly, choosing his words carefully. "This baby King," he explained, "is not like any other king. He is the Son of God, Lord of everything. One day He will be King of everything, but right now, His Father has sent him with a special purpose. His children had lost their way by following other gods. None of the men around this table," he shared, "had been believers before today." Narod explained that they had come with their own agendas and to fulfill their own curiosity. But they had experienced much more than that. God had brought them together to accomplish His plan. No one here could have shared this truth prior to today, but they were all educated and influential men, and seeing the prophecies fulfilled had convinced their minds and opened their hearts. They now knew this was the one true God, and just as all previous predictions had come true, so too would the future prophecy. The Almighty had a great purpose for His Son. He had come as a sacrifice.

For a moment Sun-Lin was speechless. Gathering his thoughts, he said, "This God loved the children of the Earth so much that He would send His Son on a mission of sacrifice so that He could reunite with them. Was there no other way?"

Narod's expression grew more sombre. "The price of redemption from sin is death," he explained. "The prophecies made it clear. One day, Jesus was going to die for each of them."

Looking past the men to the little baby asleep in his mother's arms, Sun-Lin realized that he was looking at the face of an amazing God. It would be of great importance to ensure that the facts be recorded so that others might know of this God the way Sun-Lin now knew Him. This God had come to save His people rather than be served by them.

This realization rejuvenated Sun-Lin. With a new sense of commitment, he drew close to his grandfather and the group of men. Now impressed with the desire to share all he had learned about this amazing God and His gift with his family and friends at home, he was keen to learn everything. He would document this miraculous moment and the stories of each traveller's search for the one true God in the Emperor's history books so that all would know about Him. Could it be that he, Sun-Lin, had been born with a purpose as well?

By the time they are ready to leave Bethlehem, Sun-Lin had learned much about the prophets from the assembly of men at the inn. He had arrived to pay tribute to the baby Jesus on behalf of the Emperor, but more importantly, he had given him his heart as a believer.

Tariq

Tariq was awestruck by the tremendous effort this Almighty was willing to give to restore His connection with His people. It was clear that everything he had studied about this great God was indeed true, and not to be taken lightly. All along this journey when things had gone wrong and his plans had gone awry, Tariq had doubted the involvement of this God. In fact, he had been sure that he wasn't part of this. As it turned out, the freak unseasonable storm and trouble of every nature had been for a purpose. The fact that others had been called to search out this baby, and with divine timing been able to gather together to compare and confirm their stories, was incredibly compelling to Tariq. As they had narrated their individual journeys, each had wondered anew about a God so powerful that He could give men ideas to fulfil His purpose. Recounting the numerous delays each of them had encountered, they realized that they would have probably been months apart in their arrivals had these interferences not occurred. This God had His hand on all of them the whole time, regardless of their beliefs, to ensure they would be at the chosen place, at the perfect time, to meet Him.

Again, Tariq thought back to how he had separated himself from his father in order to achieve his distinction on the counsel and yet, it had been the experience his father had provided that had ensured he had been the man selected for this magnificent appointment. Foregoing Tariq's appreciation to the point where their relationship had suffered, his father's love and desire to do what was best for his son had inevitably had the greatest impact on his life. This was but a small glimpse into the depth of the love God had for His children.

The idea of this God growing up and living among His children, guiding them and offering them counsel, seemed like a perfect way to give credibility to His love and desire for a relationship with them. With the prophecies of Jesus' birth confirmed, each man knew this was only the beginning. Filled with the conviction that the prophecies would be realized in the future, as they had been today, they reviewed the responsibilities that each of them felt led to fulfil.

Tariq's faithful servant and protector Lamir had caught up to them as they had been leaving Jerusalem and informed him of the soldiers' purpose. When Elam told of the nasty king's reputation, the men doubted the alleged reasons for the king's inquiry and they feared for Jesus' safety. When Nasir spoke of the incident in Jerusalem with Simeon and Anna at the temple, the men knew that Herod would quickly find them all. They agreed that Joseph would be wise to leave town and put a great distance between his family and Bethlehem before Herod could locate them. Tariq, sensing great fear in Herod, had been sleepless with visions of the man trying to destroy the Holy Child. He could help the family get away. Offering them his best camel and supplies, they could join him and his men for protection as they returned home via Egypt. Due to his position and power, travelling with Tariq ensured their safety. He would study when he could along the way to learn more about this incredible God and then document his learnings on his own scrolls so that other men might study and know Him as he did.

Elam

Elam shifted his posture when the morning sunlight caught his eyes. So involved had he been with the men's conversations, he had not noticed the passage of time. His cloak had slipped open from the movement and the bright light caught the shimmer of the rich fabric hidden beneath. Pulling his camel's-hair cloak back over the garment below, he took a moment to sit back. Glancing around at the humble surroundings, he realized that he had been misguided in his effort at becoming a great leader. What others had thought of him had seemed so important at the beginning of this journey, but had lost all significance at the discovery of the Christ child. Rising up from the group of men, he approached the baby Jesus sleeping soundly in his mother's arms. He had been scared of appearing weak, but here was the Lord, fragile and soft, giving Himself to become the most vulnerable of them all. Bowing down, a new sense of wonder in this God swelled up inside him. Elam didn't have any previous faith in this amazing God, but now he believed.

By lowering himself to the level of man, this God wanted to ensure that His people understood the depth of His love for them. He wanted His people to be able to trust Him. This attempt to reunite with His people wasn't wrapped in worldly trappings or intellect or one's position in society. Rather, it was simple and straightforward. God wasn't looking to impress. Although the thought of implementing all the prophecies of this incredible plan was certainly impressive, He was looking to confirm His children's faith by removing all doubt with the ultimate gift.

So where were the great leaders of these people's faith? Why weren't they here? Were they busy flouncing around in their own pomp and circumstance, like those he had left behind in the temple near his palace? Or were they waiting for someone else to come forward, ever fearful to appear the fool? Elam knew this fear. He had been so concerned with his own reputation. Were they as insecure as he? That these three small bands of men were the only ones to pay homage to the baby King was an embarrassment to all mankind. It was obviously time for a new faith.

His position in the government and the title of governor was no longer the appointment that Elam would strive for each day. The worthiest calling would be to guide the people so that they would know their one true God. Elam would go home and hire unpretentious men of the Lord to lead them in their search for a renewed faith. This God was not looking for worldly doctrine or false conviction; He was looking to become part of their lives by living at one with them. And Elam would wait expectantly, knowing that this most powerful God who could cause all of this to pass would quite surely have His hand on future events as well.

Elam now understood that the Lord had chosen this humble beginning as the essence of his belief. One day, Jesus would return to Galilee, and Elam would be waiting.

JOSEPH

JOSEPH had left Nasir and Tariq in the company of some new guests and searched out Mary and baby Jesus as soon as he had arrived at the Inn. His mind was swimming with all the knowledge Tariq had shared on the Jewish laws and the signs of the arrival of the baby Jesus, the Messiah. His doubt had disappeared on the evening of Jesus' birth with Jophar's appearance at the stable, and then Simeon in Jerusalem had confirmed his newfound understanding. But today's arrival of Tariq had given Joseph even greater confidence and reason to celebrate. Now he could return home with Mary and Jesus without fear of reprisal.

When he had returned to the main room with his wife and son, he was surprised to see Tariq deep in conversation with the other guests. When their lively conversation had abruptly halted with Jesus' appearance, Joseph knew that they too had sought the King of Kings. Catching himself holding his breath, Joseph wondered what miracle was at hand. As if on cue, the front door had opened and Jophar paraded in, leading an even more extraordinary group of foreigners that he had introduced to Joseph as men on a quest to see the King. Strangers from different ends of the Earth had just arrived simultaneously with the same purpose. Unsure of what to make of the whole astonishing affair, Joseph had stayed quiet and listened. Each man had taken tremendous risks, in reputation and life, to ascertain whether the ancient scrolls were true. He admired their devotion and wondered anew why the Lord had chosen him to be Jesus' earthly father. A simple carpenter, it seemed he had nothing to offer. Prior to Jesus' birth he had given nothing of himself to his Lord. He knew he had been so buried in his self-righteousness that he had been blind to the blessings he had been given. And yet God had been prepared for his foolishness. How else to explain why they were all gathered here on this very day?

It wasn't until Tariq questioned Joseph about his lineage that his purpose became clear. The Messiah was to be a descendant of David. The very reason Joseph had brought Mary to Bethlehem was to be counted here for the census, as he was from the House of David. His ancestry was crucial to fulfilling this prophecy. Still feeling humbled after Jophar's arrival at the stable, he thought it appropriate that he would provide this distinguished legacy passed down through the generations without it requiring any special skill on his part. After his lack of faith, he didn't want anyone to think he had been chosen for this role because of something he wasn't. He would be keeping his arrogance in check from now on.

Mary

With the men comfortably settled, Mary had finished cleaning up and sat down to rock Jesus to sleep. She had resisted heading to their room and boldly chosen to stay sitting in the main room listening to the men talk. Two of the men had obviously studied languages, including Hebrew and Greek, and the elderly man had brought along a fellow capable of translation so the group could converse with each other and with Joseph. They were all presently deep in conversation.

She was still stunned and amazed that the Son of God was peacefully slumbering cradled in her arms while great men from the far corners of the Earth laid huge offerings of gold and treasures at her feet. That his future well-being was secure was evident by the riches before her. The men took turns comparing their knowledge of the events that had unfolded and quietly bowed before Jesus in respect and adoration. That these highly educated and respected men from distant lands did not seem to question his lineage still baffled her. Nasir had told Joseph that the religious leaders at the temple had been less than impressed and far too interested in themselves to be concerned with the realization of the prophecies. She was sure that they were not alone and that most men would find the whole story impossible to believe. The initial responses of Joseph and her father were perfect examples. The questioning crowds at the temple were others.

The trip to Jerusalem had been a nostalgic journey for Mary. Carefully repositioning herself in the cart so as not to wake the baby sleeping in her arms as the mule plodded along, she had let her mind drift back to her childhood and the times she had shared a similar cart with her mother and Fatima. Wistfully she had dreamed of returning to her family, imagining the joy of raising her son with her parents close by.

The vision of her little family's return home had been revived when, following their trip to Jerusalem, Joseph had announced his plan to return to Nazareth. He was positive that the news of Simeon and Anna's announcements at the temple would travel quickly and that their hometown would welcome them with open arms and celebration. She had been less than convinced. A cold shiver ran down her spine as she remembered her father's initial response and wondered how much it would take to prove the truth to the less faithful. But now, with the vast wealth laying before her, surely there would be no question to the validity of Jesus' birthright. Wouldn't all these riches support it? No doubt Joseph was right and everyone would want to celebrate.

Jesus had long since fallen asleep in Mary's lap while she dozed. When Joseph tapped her gently on the shoulder, she was surprised to see the early dawn lighting the room. Careful not to disturb the baby, he quietly told her of the new plans that had been made.

Tariq had shared his fears of Herod with Joseph and the group and it had been decided that the little family should move on as soon as possible. Tariq would escort them to Egypt. All the trips he had made there with his father meant that he had valuable contacts that would make the transition as easy and safe as possible. To return to Nazareth would be too great a risk. Herod would eventually find Jesus and Joseph would surely come under scrutiny and possibly be jailed for thievery. Away from prying eyes they could raise Jesus out of harm's way. Mary knew that the men were right. With her dream of going home dashed, she began to weep. Feelings of loneliness washed over her. But unlike their trip to Bethlehem, this time, she would have the comfort and support of Joseph. Bending down in front of her so she could see his face, he slowly smiled. Gently he reminded her that of all people, she should never feel alone; after all, the Son of God was sleeping in her lap. Mary felt an incredible joy swell within her knowing Joseph was right. It didn't matter where they went. One day her little boy would rise up and no longer need his mother, but for now, she would store up the feelings of this little baby, warm and content in her arms.

Gabriel

Gabriel had been dancing and singing praises to God with the other angels as the dazzling star had shone beneath them. Looking down, he paused and smiled at the picture below. How he loved it when God's children realized how real their Lord was and how much a part of their lives He was.

Jophar and his simple faith had Gabriel bursting with joy. Where were the boys that had taunted Jophar now? Were they wishing they were the ones with the cleft lip, or were they still wondering why God had chosen Jophar instead of them? His deformity had helped Jophar grow up wise and strong in character. It had placed him in his father's company where he could learn about his Lord. And it had placed him out on the hill with the sheep and goats that night. The boy whom the world had considered punished or forgotten by God had actually been blessed beyond measure.

And Nasir, with his steadfast trust in God, had finally seen the Lord's hand in Jophar's life. All the years of watching his youngest son suffer paled instantly in the radiance of the Almighty's plan. Nasir finally understood that blessings weren't always easy to see. At this, Gabriel's delight was immeasurable.

The group of strangers that had gathered at the inn had formed an allegiance of wise and powerful men committed to following the Lord's will. Each of them had realized that the hand of an amazing God had put them there. Humbled, they wondered why God had selected them to be a part of this momentous event. They had committed their hearts to their roles they felt led to play as the future unfolded.

Sun-Lin had had no desire to spend months alone with his aging grandfather but had agreed only to get away from his boring schooling. He would return home with a vision and purpose to see the history of the Lord's birth recorded accurately. Those boring books would now come to life as he shared this amazing moment in time.

Tariq had virtually disowned his father, and yet it was the travel experience his father had provided that had ensured Tariq was selected for this trip. It was his own father's sacrifice that had helped Tariq understand the depth of God's love. Now he would use his contacts to ensure that Jesus would be safe in Egypt.

And Elam, desperate to be seen as a great man, would have never been aware of any of it without his faithful servant Narod. He would go home and re-examine his desire for greatness, and with the help of others he would become a servant preparing the people for their Saviour. That the Lord had used three men of no faith to secure the future of his plan had Gabriel smiling in awe.

Mary and Joseph, in that simple moment so natural for every new parent, had finally grasped the gift they had been given. With their faith set, they had silently committed to themselves, each other, and God. Their journey was just beginning.

Watching from the heavens Gabriel acknowledged this bittersweet moment as 'The Plan' finally took its last steps on its journey to completion. Gabriel knew that the waiting was almost over and that the door would soon be open for all of the Lord's children to come back to The Father. Carefully created to express His immeasurable love and divine nature, The Plan was designed to ensure that every man, woman, and child would simply have to accept His gift to be reunited with their Heavenly Father.

God had sat and mourned while witnessing His children suffer at their own hands for so long. It had been devastating to see how they took their ability to think and choose freely and entwined it with earthly sins. If not for His unremitting love, He would have simply abandoned them all. How His heart ached while He waited with open arms for each of them.

One day, not long from now, it would be finished. Here, from the humblest of beginnings, the gift of eternal life begins.

Author's Note

From the beginning, when Adam and Eve fell into sin, God had been planning to reunite with His children. The birth of Jesus and the Christmas story is man's first glimpse at the realization of a plan that had been foretold to generations prior, a plan that would manifest thirty-three years later in the death and resurrection of Jesus, God's own son, and the gift of salvation. This is the story of hope and the ultimate gift of irrevocable love. From the rich to the poor, the powerful to the meek, this hope is the perfect Christmas gift for everyone. I pray your hearts and minds are open to receive His Gift today.

www.ingramcontent.com/pod-product-compliance
Ingram Content Group UK Ltd.
Pitfield, Milton Keynes, MK11 3LW, UK
UKHW020416250726
13967UKWH00007B/2680

9 781773 705576